Barocke Tänze
für Altblockflöte
zusätzlich mit 2. Stimme

Baroque Dances
for treble recorder
with additional 2nd part

Danses baroques
pour flûte à bec alto
avec 2nde partie supplémentaire

herausgegeben von / edited by / édités par
Rainer Butz und / and / et Hans Magolt

ED 20869
ISMN 979-0-001-17215-8

Cover: Karin Schliehe und Bernhard Mark

Komponisten auf dem Cover:
G. F. Händel (oben links), J. S. Bach (oben Mitte),
C. Monteverdi (oben rechts), H. Purcell (unten links), J. B. Lully (unten rechts)

www.schott-music.com

Mainz · London · Madrid · Berlin · New York · Paris · Prague · Tokyo · Toronto
© 2014 SCHOTT MUSIC GmbH & Co. KG, Mainz · Printed in Germany

Branle simple und Branle gay

De Post (Danserye, Antwerpen 1551)

♩ = ca. 72, Vorspiel: 2 Takte

Arrangements: Rainer Butz

Tielman Susato
~1500–1561

Branle gay

Branle double

Bransle (Terpsichore, Wolfenbüttel 1612)

♩ = ca. 68, Vorspiel: 2 Takte mit Auftakt

Michael Praetorius
1571–1621

Branle gay
(Neuf basses dances deux branles etc., Paris 1530)

Pierre Attaingnant
~1494–1551

♩. = ca. 68, Vorspiel: 4 Takte mit Auftakt

4

Basse dance
(Neuf basses dances deux branles etc, Paris 1530)

Pierre Attaingnant
~1494–1551

♩ = ca. 116, Vorspiel: 2 Takte

Ronde und Saltarelle
Ronde und Hupfauf (Danserye, Antwerpen 1551)

Tielman Susato
~1550–1561

♩ = ca. 128, Vorspiel: 2 Takte

© 2014 Schott Music GmbH & Co. KG, Mainz

Saltarelle

Basse dance

La mourisque / Mohrentanz (Danserye, Antwerpen 1551)

Tielman Susato
~1500–1561

♩ = ca. 80, Vorspiel: 2 Takte

Basse dance und Nachtanz

Bergerette „Dont vient cela" und Reprise (Danserye, Antwerpen 1551)

Tielman Susato
~1500–1561

♩ = ca. 144, Vorspiel: 6 Viertel

Reprise

Pavane und Galliarde

Belle qui tiens ma vie (Orchésographie, Langres 1589)

Thoinot Arbeau
1520–1595

Pavane
Pavane de Spaigne (Terpsichore, Wolfenbüttel 1612)

Michael Praetorius
1571–1621

♩ = ca. 64, Vorspiel: 2 Takte

Galliarde
Galiarda (Fitzwilliam Virginal Book, ~1550–1620)

John Bull
~1562–1628

♩ = ca. 152, Vorspiel: 2 Takte

10

Pavane

Pavan of my Lord Lumley (Fitzwilliam Virginal Book, ~1550–1620)

John Bull
~1562–1628

♩ = ca. 52, Vorspiel: 2 Takte

Galliarde

Wer wird mich herzen (Lautenbuch)

Johan Thysius
1621–1653

♩ = ca. 168, Vorspiel: 2 Takte

Galliarde

Tanzen und Springen (Lustgarten neuer teutscher Tänze, 1601)

Hans Leo Haßler
1562–1612

♩ = ca. 172, Vorspiel: 2 Takte

Tanz und Nachtanz

nach Art von Allemande und Tripla (Nürnberg ~1600)

Valentin Haußmann
~1570–1614

♩ = ca. 144, Vorspiel: 2 Takte mit Auftakt

Nachtanz

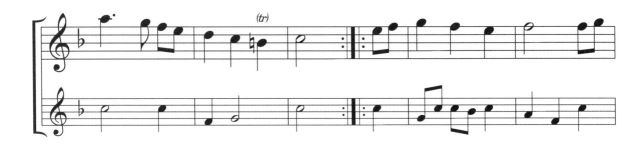

Siciliana

Moresca aus der Oper „L'Orfeo" (1607)

Claudio Monteverdi
1567–1643

♩. = ca. 56, Vorspiel: 2 Takte mit Auftakt

Allemande und Tripla

(Banchetto musicale, Leipzig 1617)

Johann Hermann Schein
1586–1630

♩ = ca. 140, Vorspiel: 2 Takte mit Auftakt

Courante

The Old Spagnoletta (Fitzwilliam Virginal Book, ~1550–1620)

Giles Farnaby
~1563–1640

♩ = ca. 180, Vorspiel: 2 Takte mit Auftakt

16

Allemande

Nun will der Lenz uns grüßen (vor 1600)

♩ = ca. 120, Vorspiel: 2 Takte mit Auftakt

nach einem alten Reigenlied
aus Deutschland

Courante

Wie schön blüht uns der Maien

♩. = ca. 56, Vorspiel: 2 Takte mit Auftakt

Heidelberger Liederblatt
1602

Courante
bei Michael Praetorius (Terpsichore, Wolfenbüttel 1612)

Pierre Francisque Caroubel
~1560–1611

♩. = ca. 60, Vorspiel: 2 Takte mit Auftakt

Sarabande
aus der Suite in d-Moll für Cembalo HWV 437 (vor 1733)

Georg Friedrich Händel
1685–1759

♩ = ca. 68, Vorspiel: 2 Takte mit 3 Vierteln Auftakt

18

Sarabande

Arie „Lascia ch'io pianga" aus der Oper „Rinaldo" (1711)

Georg Friedrich Händel
1685–1759

♩ = ca. 68, Vorspiel: 2 Takte mit 1 Viertel Auftakt

Fine

© 2014 Schott Music GmbH & Co. KG, Mainz

D.C. al Fine

Gigue

Down the green fields, we'll jig it

♩. = ca. 64, Vorspiel: 2 Takte

Volksweise
aus England

Fine

D.C. al Fine con rip.

Gigue

Ich spring' an diesem Ringe

♩. = ca. 60, Vorspiel: 2 Takte mit Auftakt

Lochamer Liederbuch
~1452–1460

Sarabande
Air tendre für Cembalo

Jean-Baptiste Lully
1632–1687

♩ = ca. 68, Vorspiel: 2 Takte

Marsch

Trauermarsch aus dem Oratorium „Saul" (1739)

Georg Friedrich Händel
1685–1759

♩ = ca. 60, Vorspiel: 1 Takt mit Auftakt

Menuett

Arie „How blest are shepherds" aus der Oper „King Arthur" (1691)

Henry Purcell
1659–1695

♩ = ca. 112, Vorspiel: 2 Takte

Menuett

(Clavierbüchlein für Anna Magdalena Bach, Leipzig 1725, BWV Anh.114)

Christian Petzold
1677–1733

♩ = ca. 112, Vorspiel: 2 Takte

Chaconne
aus der Oper „The Fairy Queen" (1692)

Henry Purcell
1659–1695

♩ = ca. 76, Vorspiel: 2 Takte

Passepied
aus der Oper „L'Europe galante" (1697)

André Campra
1660–1744

♪ = ca. 152, Vorspiel: 2 Takte mit Auftakt

Gavotte
aus der Orchestersuite Nr.3 D-Dur BWV 1068 (1731)

Johann Sebastian Bach
1685–1750

♩ = ca. 60, Vorspiel: 2 Takte mit 2 Vierteln Auftakt

Hornpipe

Duett „Shepherd leave decoying" aus der Oper „King Arthur" (1691)

♩ = ca. 76, Vorspiel: 2 Takte

Henry Purcell
1659–1695

Schott Music, Mainz 53 837

Pavane (Abraham Bosse 1635)

Ludwig XIV. tanzt Menuett (Pierre Landry 1682)

Sarabande (aus Gregorio Lambranzi: Neue und Curieuse Theatralische Tantz=Schul, Nürnberg 1716)

Inhalt / Contents / Contenu

Barocke Grifftabelle

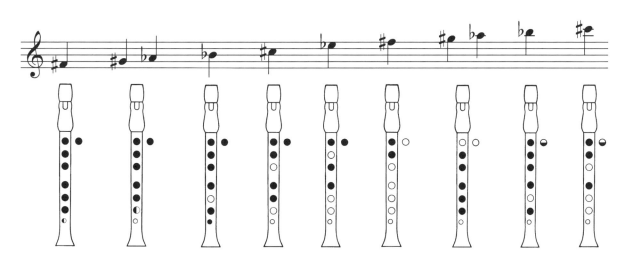

Menuett (aus Pierre Rameau: Le maître à danser, Paris 1734)

Referenz (Christoph Murer, um 1600)

Referenz (aus Th. Arbeau: Orchésographie, 1589)

Contents

All Photos by Steve Wright
Music Transcribed by Roger Day
Music Processed by Musicprint Ltd
Folio Produced by Ron Fry
Designed and Printed by Panda Press

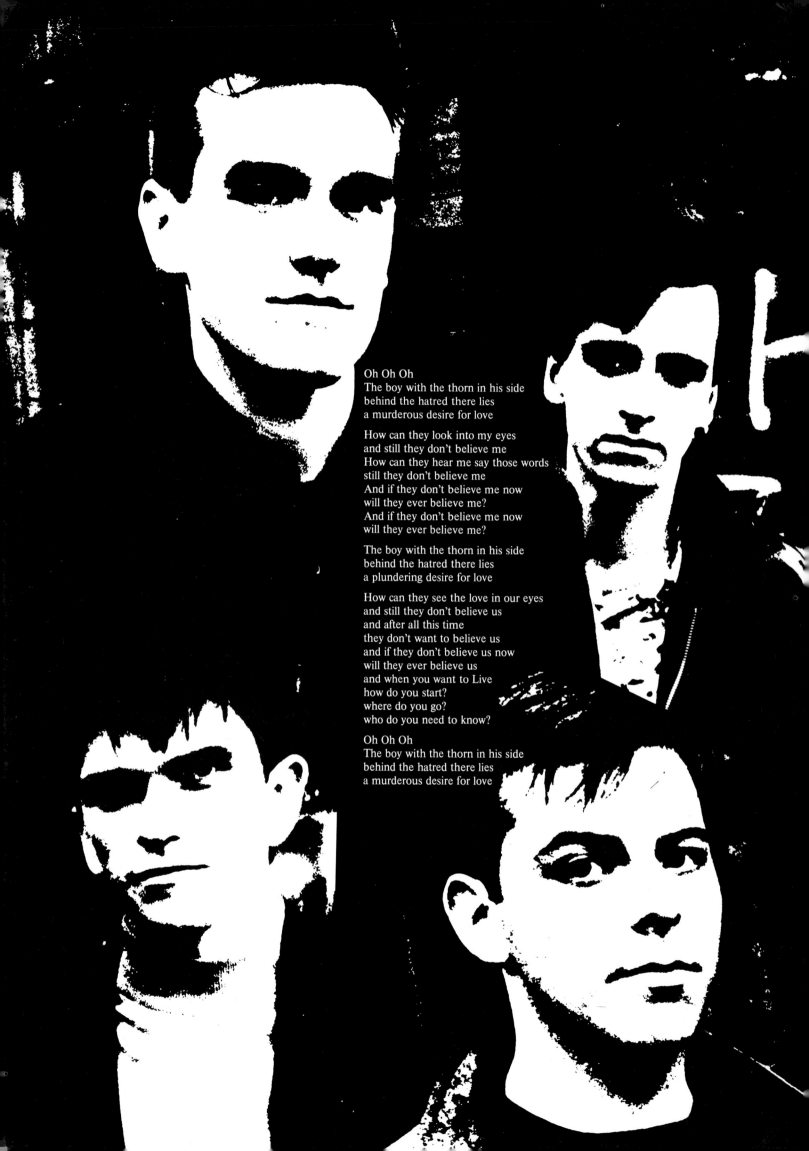

Oh Oh Oh
The boy with the thorn in his side
behind the hatred there lies
a murderous desire for love

How can they look into my eyes
and still they don't believe me
How can they hear me say those words
still they don't believe me
And if they don't believe me now
will they ever believe me?
And if they don't believe me now
will they ever believe me?

The boy with the thorn in his side
behind the hatred there lies
a plundering desire for love

How can they see the love in our eyes
and still they don't believe us
and after all this time
they don't want to believe us
and if they don't believe us now
will they ever believe us
and when you want to Live
how do you start?
where do you go?
who do you need to know?

Oh Oh Oh
The boy with the thorn in his side
behind the hatred there lies
a murderous desire for love

THE BOY WITH A THORN IN HIS SIDE

Words and Music by
MORRISSEY and JOHNNY MARR

lieve me now will they ev will they ev - er be-lieve me? Oh

(INTRO.)

Oh Oh Oh

CHORUS: The boy with the thorn in his side
           behind the hatred there lies
           a plundering desire for love

VERSE 2:   How can they see the love in our eyes
           and still they don't believe us
           and after all this time
           they don't want to believe us
           and if they don't believe us now
           will they ever believe us
           and when you want to Live
           how do you start?
           where do you go?
           who do you need to know?

INTRO: (Repeat)

CHORUS: (Instr.)

Sweetness, sweetness, I was only joking when I said
I'd like to smash ev'ry tooth in your head
Oh sweetness, sweetness, I was only joking when I said
by rights you should be bludgeoned in your bed
And now I know how Joan of Arc felt,
now I know how Joan of Arc felt
as the flames rose to her Roman nose
and her Walkman started to melt

Big mouth la da da da da
big mouth la da da da
big mouth strikes again
and I've got no right to take my place
with the human race
Oh oh oh oh oh
big mouth la da da da da
big mouth la da da da
big mouth strikes again
and I've got no right to take my place
with the human race

And now I know how Joan of Arc felt,
now I know how Joan of Arc felt
as the flames rose to her Roman nose
and her hearing aid started to melt.

BIGMOUTH STRIKES AGAIN

Words and Music by
MORRISSEY and JOHNNY MARR

nose and her {Walk - man / hear - ing aid} start - ed to___ melt.___

When you walk without ease
on these the very streets where you were raised
I had a really bad dream
it lasted twenty years, seven months,
and twenty seven days.

Never, never,
had no one ever,
now I'm outside your house
I'm alone,
and I'm outside your house
I hate to intrude

oh I'm alone, I'm alone
I'm alone, I'm alone
I'm alone, I'm alone
and I never, never,
had no one ever,
I never had no one ever,
I never had no one,
no one ever,
had no one ever,
I never had no one.

NEVER HAD NO ONE EVER

Words and Music by
MORRISSEY and JOHNNY MARR

ad lib. to FADE

I was minding my own business
lifting some lead off
the roof of The Holy Church,
it was worthwhile living a laughable life
just to set my eyes on the blistering sight
of a vicar in a tu-tu,
he's not strange,
he just wants to live his life this way.

A scanty bit of a thing
with a decorative ring
that wouldn't cover the head of a child
as Rose collects the money in a canister
who comes sliding down the bannister
the vicar in a tu-tu
he's not strange
he just wants to live his life this way.

The monkish Monsignor
with a head full of plaster
said, "My man, get your vile soul dry-cleaned"
as Rose counts the money in the canister
as natural as rain
he dances again
vicar in a tu-tu.

The next day in the pulpit
with Freedom and Ease
combatting ignorance, dust and disease
as Rose counts the money in the canister
as natural as rain
he dances again
the fabric of a tu-tu
any man could get used to
and I am a living sign

VICAR IN A TUTU

Words and Music by
MORRISSEY and JOHNNY MARR

I was mind-ing my busi-ness lift ing some lead off the

roof of the Ho - ly Name church, it was

worth while liv - ing a laugh-a-ble life just to

am a liv - ing sign_____ I'm a liv - ing

VERSE 2:
A scanty bit of a thing
With a decorative ring
That wouldn't cover the head of a child
As Rose collects the money in a canister
Who comes sliding down the bannister
The vicar in a tu-tu
He's not strange
He just wants to live his life this way.

VERSE 3:
The monkish Monsignor
With a head full of plaster
Said, My man, get your vile soul dry-cleaned
As Rose counts the money in the canister
As natural as rain
He dances again
Vicar in a tu-tu.

VERSE 4:
The next day in the pulpit
With Freedom and Ease
Combatting ignorance, dust and disease
As Rose counts the money in the canister
As natural as rain
He dances again
The fabric of a tu-tu
Any man could get used to
And I am a living sign.

From the Ice Age to the dole age
there is but one concern
and I have just discovered:
Some girls are bigger than others
some girls are bigger than others
some girls' mothers are bigger than
other girls' mothers
some girls are bigger than others
some girls are bigger than others
some girls' mothers are bigger than
other girls' mothers.

As Anthony said to Cleopatra
as he opened a crate of ale:
Some girls are bigger than others
some girls are bigger than others
some girls' mothers are bigger than
other girls' mothers
some girls are bigger than others
some girls are bigger than others
some girls' mothers are bigger than
other girls' mothers.

SOME GIRLS ARE BIGGER THAN OTHERS

Words and Music by
MORRISSEY and JOHNNY MARR

Take me out tonight
where there's music and there's people
who are young and alive
driving in your car
I never never want to go home
because I haven't got one
anymore

Take me out tonight
because I want to see people and I
want to see lights
driving in your car
oh please don't drop me home
because it's not my home, it's their
home, and I'm not welcome no more

And if a double decker bus
crashes into us
to die by your side
such a heavenly way to die
and if a ten ton truck
kills the both of us
to die by your side
the pleasure and the privilege is mine.

Take me out tonight
oh take me anywhere, I don't care
and in the darkened underpass
I thought, oh God, my chance has come at last
(But then a strange fear gripped me and I
just couldn't ask)

Take me out tonight
oh take me anywhere, I don't care
just drive in your car
I never want to go home
because I haven't got one
I haven't got one.

THERE IS A LIGHT THAT NEVER GOES OUT

Words and Music by
MORRISSEY and JOHNNY MARR

Dri - ving in your car, _____ I ne -

- ver, ne - ver want to go home, ___ be - cause I have - n't got one

a - ny - more. _____

And if a dou - ble deck - er bus ___

VERSE 2:
Take me out tonight
Because I want to see people and I
Want to see lights
Driving in your car
Oh please don't drop me home
Because, it's not my home, it's their
home, and I'm welcome no more.

VERSE 3:
Take me out tonight
Oh take me anywhere, I don't care
And in the darkened underpass
I thought, oh God, my chance has come at last
(But then a strange fear gripped me and I
Just couldn't ask).

VERSE 4:
Take me out tonight
Take me anywhere, I don't care
Just drive in your car
I never never want to go home
Because I haven't got one
I haven't got one.

Frankly, Mr. Shankly, this position I've held
it pays my way, but it corrodes my soul
I want to leave, you will not miss me
I want to go down in musical history

Frankly, Mr. Shankly, I'm a sickening wreck
I've got the 21st Century breathing down my neck
I must move fast, you understand me
I want to go down in celluloid history

Fame, Fame, fatal Fame
it can play hideous tricks on the brain
but still I'd rather be Famous
than righteous or holy, any day

But sometimes I'd feel more fulfilled
making Christmas cards with the mentally ill
I want to Live and I want to Love
I want to catch something that I might be ashamed of

Frankly, Mr. Shankly, this position I've held
it pays my way and it corrodes my soul
oh, I didn't realise that you wrote poetry
(I didn't realise you wrote such bloody awful poetry).

Frankly, Mr. Shankly, since you ask
you are a flatulent pain in the arse
I do not mean to be so rude
but still? I must speak frankly, Mr. Shankly.

FRANKLY, MR. SHANKLY

Words and Music by
MORRISSEY and JOHNNY MARR

you will not miss me, I want to go down in

mu - si - cal his - to - ry.

(ny)

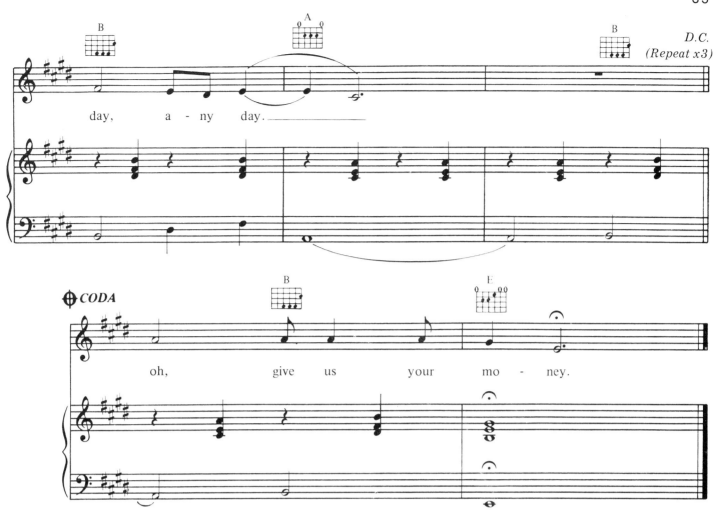

oh, give us your mo - ney.

Frankly Mr. Shankly, I'm a sickening wreck
I've got the 21st Century breathing down my neck
I must move fast, you understand me
I want to go down in celluloid history.

But sometimes, I'd feel more fulfilled
Making Christmas cards with the mentally ill
I want to live and I want to love
I want to catch something that I might be ashamed of.

Frankly Mr. Shankly, this position I've held
It pays my way and it corrodes my soul
Oh I didn't realise that you wrote poetry
(I didn't realise that you wrote such bloody awful poetry).

Frankly Mr. Shankly, since you ask
You are a flatulent pain in the arse
I do not mean to be so rude
But still, I must speak frankly, Mr. Shankly.

A dreaded sunny day
so I meet you at the cemetery gates
Keats and Yates are on your side
a dreaded sunny day
so I meet you at the cemetery gates
Keats and Yates are on your side
while Wilde is on mine
So we go inside and we gravely read the stones
all those people, all those lives
where are they now?
with loves, and hates
and passions just like mine
they were born
and then they lived
and then they died
which seems so unfair
and I want to cry
you say "ere thrice the sun hath done
salutation to the dawn"
and you claim these words as your own
but I'm well-read, have heard them said
a hundred times (maybe less, maybe more)
if you must write prose/poems
the words you use should be your own
don't plagiarise or take "on loan"
there's always someone, somewhere
with a big nose, who knows
and who trips you up and laughs
when you fall
who'll trip you up and laugh
when you fall
you say: "ere long done do does did"
words which could only be your own
you then produce the text
from whence was ripped
(some dizzy whore, 1804)

A dreaded sunny day
so let's go where we're happy
and I meet you at the cemetery gates
Keats and Yates are on your side
a dreaded sunny day
so let's go where we're wanted
and I meet you at the cemetery gates
Keats and Yates are on your side
but you lose
because Wilde is on mine.

CEMETRY GATES

Words and Music by
MORRISSEY and JOHNNY MARR

heard them said ___ a hundred times (may-be less, ___ may-be more ___)   (3.) If you

mine.

VERSE 2:
So we go inside and we gravely read the stones
All those people all those lives
Where are they now?
With loves, and hates
And passions just like mine
They were born
And then they lived
And then they died
Which seems so unfair
And I want to cry.

VERSE 3:
If you must write prose/poems
The words you use should be your own
Don't plagiarise or take "on loan"
There's always someone, somewhere
With a big nose, who knows
And who trips you up and laughs
When you fall
Who'll trip you up and laugh
When you fall.

MIDDLE:
You say 'ere long done do does did
Words which could only be your own
You then produce the text
From whence was ripped
(some dizzy whore, 1804)

VERSE 4:
A dreaded sunny day
So let's go where we're happy
And I meet you at the cemetry gates
Keats and Yeats are on your side
A dreaded sunny day
So let's go where we're wanted
And I meet you at the cemetry gates
Keats and Yeats are on your side
But you lose
Because Wilde is on mine.

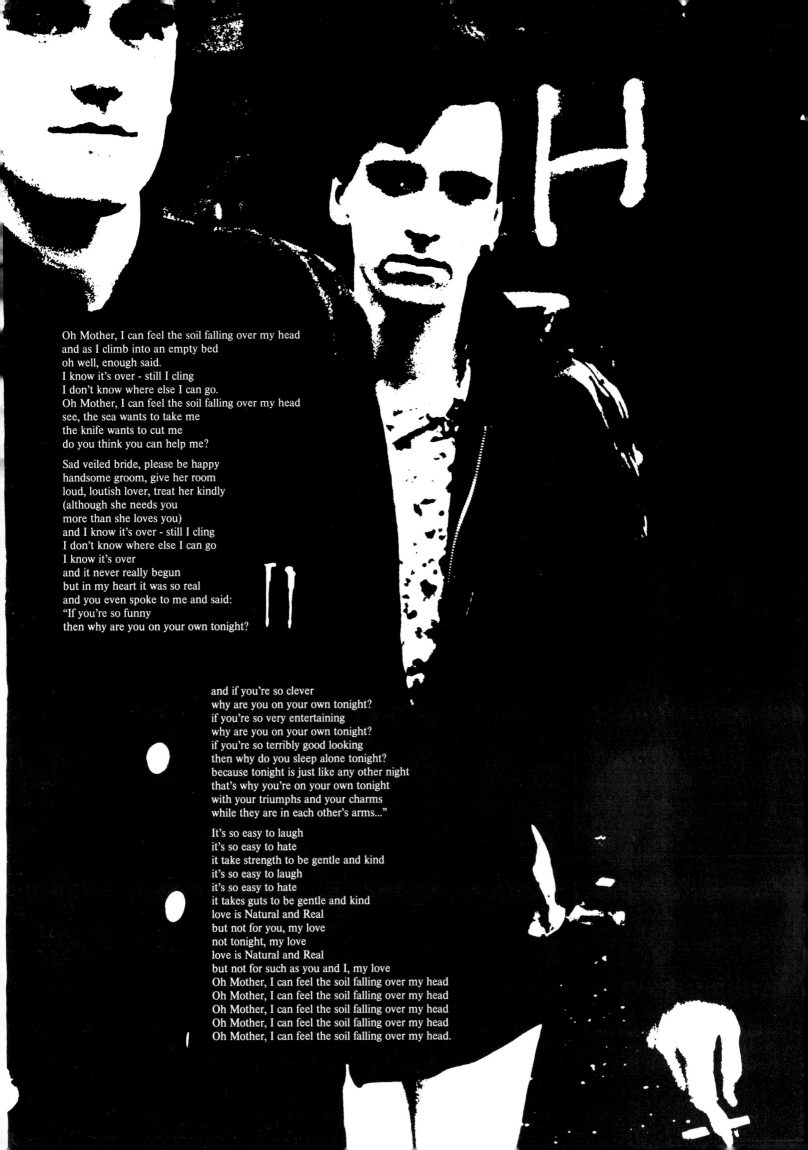

Oh Mother, I can feel the soil falling over my head
and as I climb into an empty bed
oh well, enough said.
I know it's over - still I cling
I don't know where else I can go.
Oh Mother, I can feel the soil falling over my head
see, the sea wants to take me
the knife wants to cut me
do you think you can help me?

Sad veiled bride, please be happy
handsome groom, give her room
loud, loutish lover, treat her kindly
(although she needs you
more than she loves you)
and I know it's over - still I cling
I don't know where else I can go
I know it's over
and it never really begun
but in my heart it was so real
and you even spoke to me and said:
"If you're so funny
then why are you on your own tonight?

and if you're so clever
why are you on your own tonight?
if you're so very entertaining
why are you on your own tonight?
if you're so terribly good looking
then why do you sleep alone tonight?
because tonight is just like any other night
that's why you're on your own tonight
with your triumphs and your charms
while they are in each other's arms..."

It's so easy to laugh
it's so easy to hate
it take strength to be gentle and kind
it's so easy to laugh
it's so easy to hate
it takes guts to be gentle and kind
love is Natural and Real
but not for you, my love
not tonight, my love
love is Natural and Real
but not for such as you and I, my love
Oh Mother, I can feel the soil falling over my head
Oh Mother, I can feel the soil falling over my head
Oh Mother, I can feel the soil falling over my head
Oh Mother, I can feel the soil falling over my head
Oh Mother, I can feel the soil falling over my head.

I KNOW IT'S OVER

Words and Music by
MORRISSEY and JOHNNY MARR

46

VERSE 2:
Oh mother I can feel the soil falling over my head
See, the sea wants to take me
The knife wants to cut me
Do you think you can help me?

VERSE 3:
Sad veiled bride, please be happy
Handsome groom, give her room
Loud loutish lover, treat her kindly
(Although she needs you
More than she loves you)
And I know it's over — still I cling
I don't know where else I can go
I know it's over.
(Continue 3rd time continuation bar)

VERSE 4:
If you're so funny
Then why are you on your own tonight?
And if you're so clever
Why are you on your own tonight.

VERSE 5:
If you're so very entertaining
Why are you on your own tonight?
If you're so terribly good looking
Then why do you sleep alone tonight?
(Continue 5th time bar)

Farewell to this lands cheerless marshes
hemmed in like a boar between arches
her very Lowness with her head in a sling
I'm truly sorry - but it sounds like a wonderful thing
dear Charles, don't you ever crave
to appear on the front of the Daily Mail
dressed in your Mother's bridal veil?

So, I checked all the registered historical facts
and I was shocked into shame to discover
how I'm the 18th pale descendant
of some old queen or other
has the world changed, or have I changed?
has the world changed, or have I changed?
as some 9-year old tough peddles drugs
(I never even knew what drugs were)

And so, I broke into the Palace
with a sponge and a rusty spanner
she said: "Eh, I know you, and you cannot sing"
I said: "that's nothing - you should hear me play piano"

We can go for a walk where it's quiet and dry
and we can talk about precious things
but when you're tied to your Mothers' apron
no one talks about castration

We can go for a walk where it's quiet and dry
and we can talk about precious things
like love and law and poverty
these are the things that kill me

We can go for a walk where it's quiet and dry
and we can talk about precious things
but the rain that flattens my hair
these are the things that kill me

Passes the Pub that saps your body
and the church who'll snatch your money
the Queen is dead, boys
and it's so lonely on a limb
Passed the pub that wrecks your body
and the church - all they want is your money
the Queen is dead, boys
you can trust me, boys

life is very long, when you're lonely
life is very long, when you're lonely
life is very long, when you're lonely
life is very long, when you're lonely.

THE QUEEN IS DEAD

Words and Music by
MORRISSEY and JOHNNY MARR

Fare-well _____ to this land's cheer-less marsh-es, hemmed in like a boar be-tween arch-es, her ve-ry low-ness with her head in a sling _

Life is ve - ry long _____ when you're lone - ly.

We can go for a walk where it's quiet and dry
And we can talk about precious things
Like love and law and poverty
These are the things that kill me
We can go for a walk where it's quiet and dry
And we can talk about precious things
But the rain that flattens my hair
These are the things that kill me.

Printed in England
Panda Press · Haverhill · Suffolk · 11/86